UNDER THE HOOD

HOW CARS WORK AND HOW TO KEEP THEM WORKING

WRITTEN AND ILLUSTRATED
BY
ROBIN LAWRIE

PANTHEON BOOKS

All rights reserved under International and Pan-American Copyright Conventions. Published in the United States by Pantheon Books, a division of Random House, Inc. Originally published in Great Britain as *Under the Bonnet* by Abelard-Schuman Ltd., London.

Library of Congress Cataloging in Publication Data

Lawrie, Robin.   Under the Hood.
Summary: Explains how the engine, cooling system, brakes, and other parts of a car function and demonstrates what happens if they are not cared for properly.
  1. Automobiles — Maintenance and repair — Juvenile literature. [1. Automobiles — Maintenance and repair] I. Title.
TL152.L33   629.28'8'22   72-7627
ISBN 0-394-82603-5

Manufactured in the United States of America

Cars are very useful things and it is worth caring for them to keep them at their best.

This is a story about two men with cars. One kept his car in good order. The other did not.

But before the story, it is important to see how cars work.

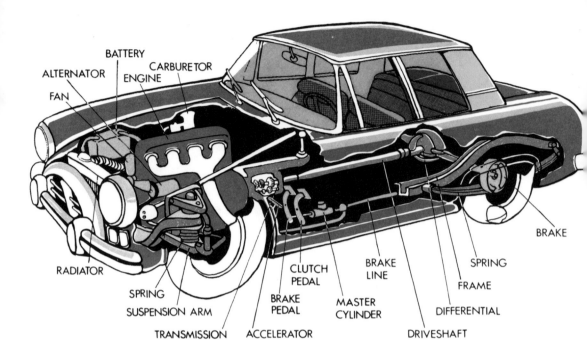

BATTERY
ALTERNATOR
CARBURETOR
ENGINE
FAN
BRAKE
RADIATOR
SPRING
SUSPENSION ARM
CLUTCH
PEDAL
BRAKE
LINE
SPRING
FRAME
TRANSMISSION
BRAKE
PEDAL
ACCELERATOR
MASTER
CYLINDER
DRIVESHAFT
DIFFERENTIAL

Here is a picture of a car with part of the outside cut away. All the important parts are labeled. It will be necessary to turn back to this page from time to time.

The bottom part of the engine of this car is like the pedals and crank of a bicycle, but instead of two legs to drive one crank, it has four pistons to drive two cranks joined together.

This is how the engine would look if it had some of the outside cut away.

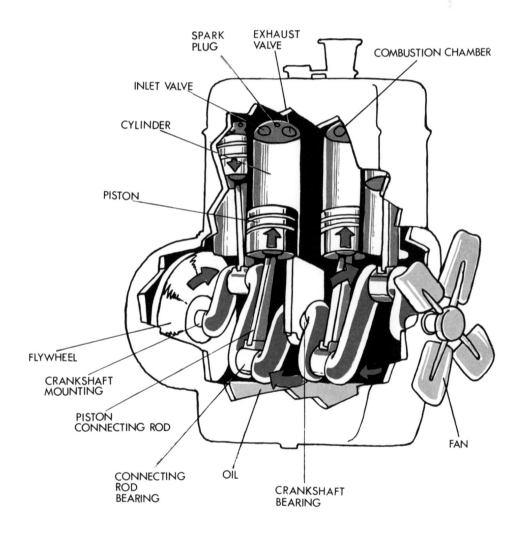

SPARK PLUG
EXHAUST VALVE
COMBUSTION CHAMBER
INLET VALVE
CYLINDER
PISTON
FLYWHEEL
CRANKSHAFT MOUNTING
PISTON CONNECTING ROD
CONNECTING ROD BEARING
OIL
CRANKSHAFT BEARING
FAN

5

The power to drive the pistons down the cylinder, so as to turn the crankshaft, begins in the carburetor, shown on page 4. Here is a cross-section of the carburetor. Its main job is to mix the gasoline with air, turning it into a spray or vapor. Gasoline alone will not burn, and burning is needed to provide power.

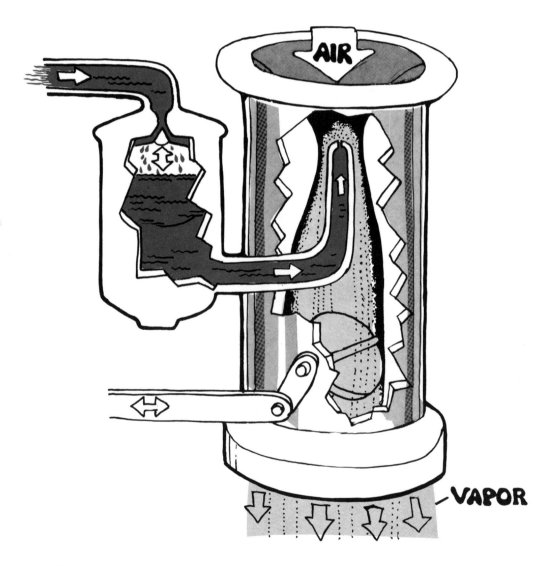

The vapor is sucked into the top of the engine through a "door" called the intake valve just as the piston is going down (drawing 1). The turning crankshaft triggers a mechanism which closes the valve to trap the vapor, and as the crankshaft continues to turn, the piston rises, squeezing the vapor into a small space (drawing 2) and compressing it. Just before the piston is as high as it will go, an electrical charge makes the spark plugs spark, causing the vapor to burn. The burning drives the piston down again with great force (drawing 3). In drawing 4 we see the piston rising again. The exhaust valve has now been opened and the smoke from the burning is driven out into the exhaust pipe. These events — called the combustion cycle — happen thousands of times every minute.

This drawing shows the order in which the events just described actually happen. Each piston is shown at a different stage. There is always one piston providing the power to force the others through the various stages.

As the pistons rise and fall, they rub against the cylinder walls, and the piston connecting rods rub against their mountings. All these parts would wear away if something were not done about it. The answer is lubrication. Here is a diagram of how it works.

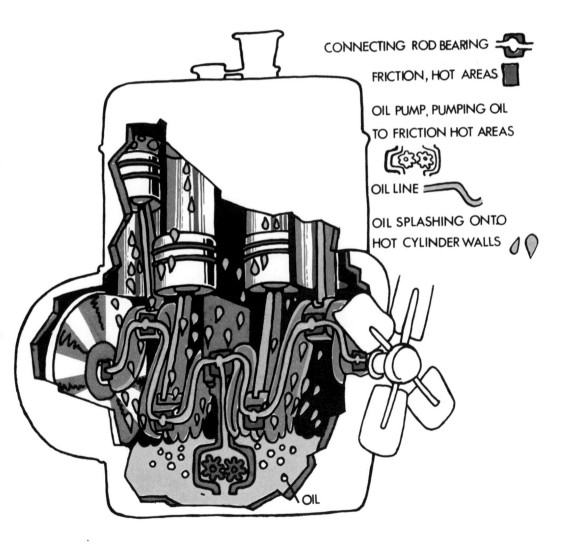

CONNECTING ROD BEARING

FRICTION, HOT AREAS

OIL PUMP, PUMPING OIL
TO FRICTION HOT AREAS

OIL LINE

OIL SPLASHING ONTO
HOT CYLINDER WALLS

OIL

A great deal of heat is caused by the burning, so there is a simple cooling system, shown below. Passages are cast in the engine and pass all around the hottest areas. They link up with a hose which leads back to the radiator. The radiator, which sits between the engine and the front of the car, is a series of small tubes with gaps between. Water from the radiator is pumped through the passages in the engine to cool it and then returns. The water is now warmer than it was and is cooled down again by air rushing between the small tubes. To help the air through when the car is not moving and the engine is running, there is a fan between the engine and the radiator.

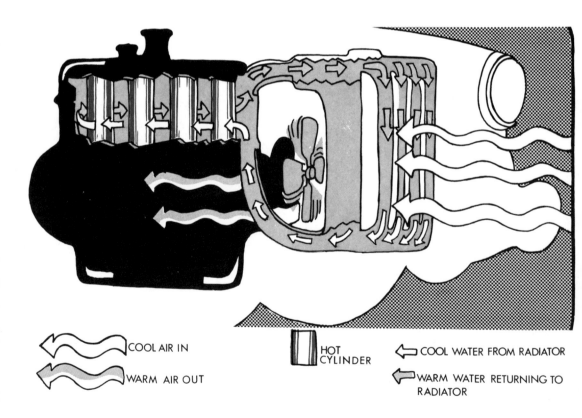

COOL AIR IN

WARM AIR OUT

HOT CYLINDER

COOL WATER FROM RADIATOR

WARM WATER RETURNING TO RADIATOR

The journey of the engine power to the wheels begins with the clutch which is directly behind the engine and which enables the driver to disconnect engine and transmission. It consists of three adjacent plates: the flywheel (1) attached to the end of the crankshaft (2), the asbestos-covered friction plate (3) and the steel pressure plate with springs attached (4). A shaft from the transmission (layshaft, 5) passes through 3 and 4. When the driver wants to move, he pushes down the clutch pedal (6), chooses a gear, then lets in the clutch. The springs push 3 against 1 and they rub together until the clutch pedal is up again and the springs are pressing the flywheel, friction plate, and steel pressure plate hard against each other. Then 1 and 3 turn together, power is sent back to the wheels, and the car moves. Whenever the driver changes gear, the process is repeated. (Below left — clutch out. Below right — clutch in.)

 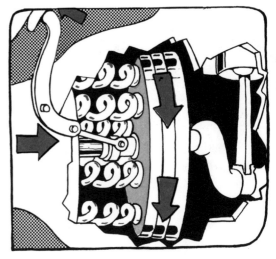

The transmission enables the driver to make the best use of the engine's power and is located behind the clutch, (see page 4). It contains three shafts. One is the layshaft, one is the driveshaft which passes the power on to the back wheels, and the third serves to connect the two in such a way that different gears can be used for different purposes. (The gears in use are shown in red.) As higher gears are used, the engine speed — that is, the number of combustion cycles per minute — is lower, but the car moves faster. (See examples below.)

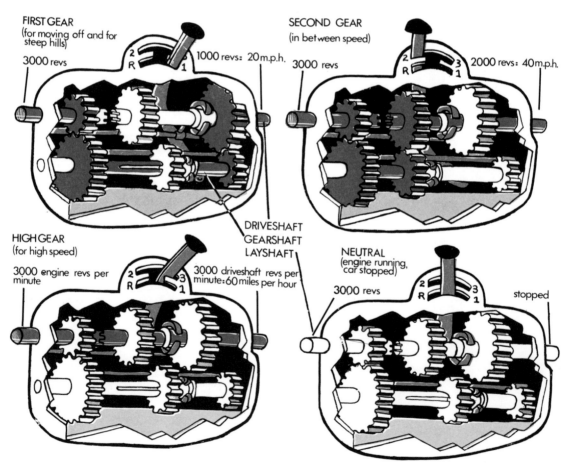

FIRST GEAR
(for moving off and for steep hills)

3000 revs

1000 revs: 20 m.p.h.

SECOND GEAR
(in between speed)

3000 revs

2000 revs: 40 m.p.h.

DRIVESHAFT
GEARSHAFT
LAYSHAFT

HIGH GEAR
(for high speed)

3000 engine revs per minute

3000 driveshaft revs per minute: 60 miles per hour

NEUTRAL
(engine running, car stopped)

3000 revs

stopped

From the transmission, the power passes via the driveshaft to the differential, whose job is to transfer power evenly to both the back wheels. The ring gear (1) in the differential is turned by the driveshaft (2). Each part of the frame (3 and 4) has a pinion gear (5 and 6) which revolves with the ring gear turning the two differential gears (7 and 8). But as long as the car is moving in a straight line, the pinion gears do not revolve. However, when, for example, the car goes into a sharp right-hand turn and the left back wheel has to make more revolutions than the right one, differential gear 8 has to revolve faster than differential gear 7. Only then do the pinion gears start to turn on their frame.

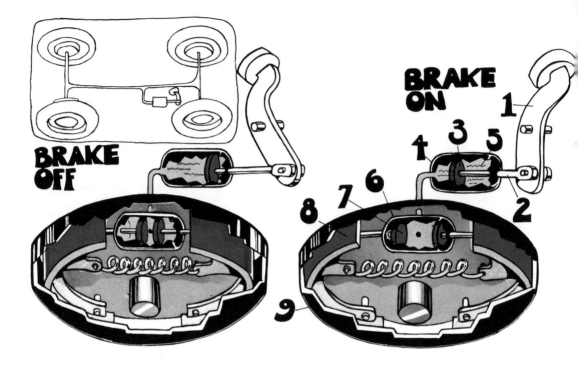

Here are the brakes. When the brake pedal (1) is pushed down, it moves a rod (2) which pushes a piston (3) along a cylinder (4) filled with a special liquid (5). The liquid is forced into a line, also containing liquid, and pressure is built up. This pressure is passed on into four more lines each leading to a "slave" cylinder (6) at each wheel, so called because it obeys every impulse of pressure.

The pressure then forces the slave's two pistons (7) against the brake shoes (8), which in turn press against the revolving brake drum (9), which is attached to the wheel itself. The wheels turn more slowly and the car comes to a stop.

14

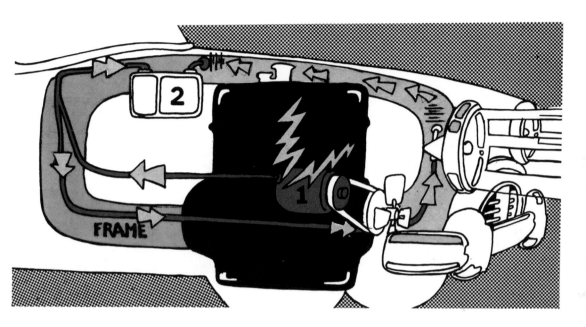

Electricity is an important part of a car. It does many jobs and two main ones are providing for the lights and the spark plugs. Electricity is like a line of men side by side in a tunnel (the wire) passing a heavy weight (electricity) from one to another until it gets into a narrower tunnel with smaller men inside (thin filament wire in bulb). The weight must still be passed on, however, and the little men get very tired and hot — white hot, in fact, which is why electric light bulbs glow.

The drawing above shows how current passes from the alternator (1) to the battery (2) which then passes the electricity on to the lights. After it has passed through the filaments, it "grounds" — shown in the picture as |ı||ı||ı — onto the frame of the car and returns to the battery through the battery's ground lead.

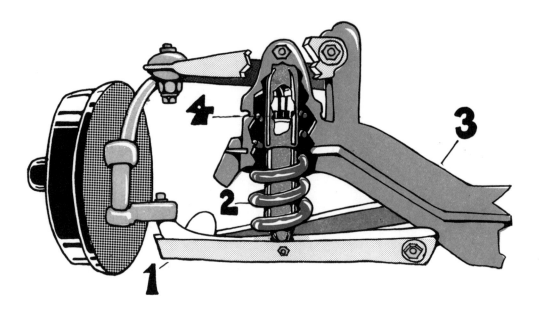

The car must go smoothly over bumps and at the same time the wheels must hold firmly to the road. To achieve this, every car has a "suspension" system. This is composed of various arms and springs between the wheels and the frame. The wheels are each attached to the two suspension arms which in turn are fixed to the frame. As the picture shows, the lower arm (1) has an attached spring (2) the other end of which joins onto the frame (3). As the car goes along, all its weight is carried by the spring which absorbs the bumps. Inside the spring is the shock absorber (4) which keeps the spring under control, forcing the wheel to stick to the road. When making a sharp turn on a rough road, if there were no shock absorbers, the inside wheels would bounce off the ground as the weight shifted to the outside wheels. Also, in straight ahead driving, if there were no shock absorbers the wheels would continue bouncing after hitting a bump. The red area is the frame and does not move with the bumps. The gray areas are suspension parts and do move with the bumps.

Mr. Brown and Mr. Smith both had cars like the one described. Mr. Smith took care of his but Mr. Brown never gave his any attention at all, and never even had it serviced at a garage. Mr. Smith was a careful road user — Mr. Brown was just the opposite.

Here is Mr. Brown at the side of the road — a place where he spends a lot of his time. He is peering into the engine, which has become overheated. The hose described on page 10 has split with age, but he doesn't notice this. Mr. Smith, who happened to be passing, stops and gives him a can of water so that he is able to refill his radiator. (Careful Mr. Smith always carries a can of water.)

With his radiator filled, Mr. Brown drives off toward the highway. But he is so careless, he has ignored a "no entry" sign, and finds himself driving up an exit ramp. Luckily he manages to turn around before there is an accident.

He drives on, but he is in for more trouble.

A tire is normally a little flat where it touches the ground. But Mr. Brown's tire is much flatter than it should be. He hasn't checked the air for a long time. As he drives along, the strengthening fabric inside the sidewall is becoming so hot that it is separating from the rubber. And then, of course, a blowout! The tire cannot take any more. Mr. Brown loses control and skids all over the road. He manages to reach the side of the highway and stops to change the tire.

Mr. Brown has had enough of the highway. He turns onto a side road, still going too fast. The road is narrow, and around a turn he meets a party of riders.

He blows his horn wildly, terrifying the horses, who prance all over the road. Fortunately, none of them is hit.

Mr. Brown drives on — fast.

The side road is bumpy as well as narrow, and the bumps show
up another defect caused by carelessness. The shock absorbers
(page 16) are hopelessly worn, so that the springs are letting the
wheels bounce freely. Mr. Brown goes around a bumpy right-hand
corner too fast, the inside wheels start to bounce up and down,
and he runs off the road into a ditch. Luckily, Mr. Smith comes
along and tows him out.

By now it is getting dark. Mr. Brown switches on his lights, but the protective covering (insulation) on one of the wires has worn right off, allowing the electricity to escape into the frame, blowing a fuse instead of passing through the headlights. The result — only one light, a sidelight! He is almost hit by another car when the driver mistakes him for a motorcycle and misjudges the gap while overtaking a truck.

A few days later Mr. Brown is once more driving happily along, ignoring the warning dials and the strange noises his car is making. Mr. Brown has forgotten that old oil loses its ability to lubricate anything, and gets very dirty as well. Engine oil should be changed every 3,000 miles or so, but Mr. Brown's oil has been at the bottom of his engine for about 14,000 miles, and is useless. The dirt in it has been wearing away the parts that rub together, for example, the cylinder walls. When oil gets very hot it becomes thin, and can seep through spaces it couldn't penetrate before. Mr. Brown's car has overheated again (page 17) and the thinned-out oil is seeping up between the pistons and the cylinders, and is being burned with the gasoline vapor, producing a thick blue smoke. Before long all the oil has burned away. The metal parts are scraping dryly against each other, becoming very hot. In fact some of them are beginning to weaken and crumble.

Then it happens!

One of the pistons gets stuck in a cylinder, due to lack of lubrication. The connecting rod, which joins the piston to the crankshaft (page 5) breaks and punches a hole in the side of the engine.

Three weeks later, with a new engine purring happily under the hood, Mr. Brown is tearing up a hill, thoroughly enjoying himself. But suddenly, although the engine is revving faster, the car is going slower. The clutch plate and springs (page 11) have worn out and the clutch is slipping. Mr. Brown wishes he had listened to Mr. Smith, who advised a new clutch while the engine was being replaced.

MR. SMITH
CHECKS HIS
BRAKES TWICE
A YEAR

He manages to crawl over the crest of the hill, and starts to coast down the other side. He presses the brake pedal, but — nothing happens! One of the connecting tubes on the brake line has rotted away and when Mr. Brown stamped on the brake, it burst.

As well as making use of the car's power in order to go faster,
the gears can also use this power to slow down.

The driver does this by selecting a lower gear than is normally suitable for the speed at that moment, but to use the power, the friction plate must be in good condition to take the strain. Mr. Brown suddenly remembers all this, puts his car into second gear, but he lets the clutch out too quickly, and BANG! the whole clutch mechanism goes. He manages to steer the car off the road, and brings it to a halt by hitting a tree.

Poor Mr. Brown! His car is in such a bad state that it isn't even fit to be towed. The back wheels lock, there is a deafening screech of tires and the axle is torn out. The rear of the car drags along the ground. Mr. Brown is angry with the driver of the towtruck.

The driver explains that the oil in the differential (page 13) had leaked out through a seal, and with no oil to protect them, the gear teeth had broken off, jamming the ring gear and stopping it entirely.

Later on, when the car is repaired, Mr. Brown decides to turn over a new leaf. He becomes good friends with his mechanic, and also with Mr. Smith. From now on, he will take proper care of his car.